The Body in Action

Eating

Claire Llewellyn

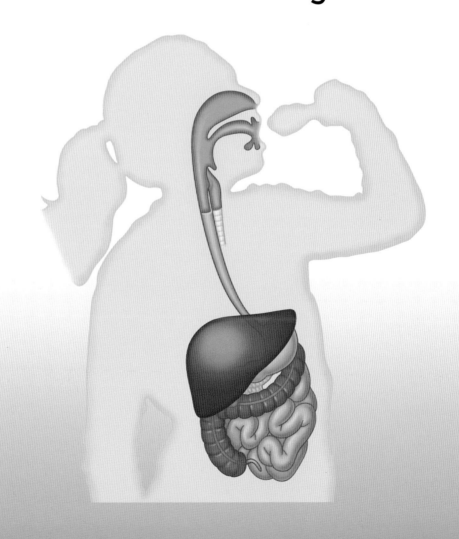

Titles in this series:
Eating
Moving
Seeing
Thinking and Feeling

Produced for A & C Black by
Bailey Publishing Associates Ltd
11a Woodlands
Hove BN3 6TJ

Editors: Alex Woolf and Jason Hook
Designer: Stonecastle Graphics
Artwork: Michael Courtney
Picture research and commissioned
photography: Ilumi Image Research
Consultant: Dr Kate Barnes

First published in 2004 by
A & C Black Publishers Ltd, 37 Soho Square,
London W1D 3QZ
www.acblack.com

A CIP catalogue record for this book is available
from the British Library.

ISBN 0 7136 63359

A & C Black uses paper produced with elemental
chlorine-free pulp, harvested from managed
sustainable forests.

Printed in Hong Kong
by Wing King Tong.

Picture Acknowledgements:
Corbis: 8; Nathan Benn: 15, 18; Mark E.
Gibson: 28; Owen Franken: 22;
Getty Images: Josef Peter Frankhauser: 5t;
Brian Hagiwara: 4; Philip Lee Harvey: 5b; Holly
Harris: 29b; David Madison: 12;
Zul Mukhida: 24;
Science Photo Library: 20; 29t;
BSIP/Margiaux: 16; Martyn F. Chillmaid: 10;
Sheila Terry: 26.

Contents

Why you need to eat

YOU NEED to eat to stay alive! Food provides the energy you need each day to breathe, move, think and keep warm. The food you eat contains goodness that your body uses. Food helps you to grow. It also helps to keep every part of your body running smoothly.

Food also gives you your 'get up and go'. Without plenty of food and water, your body works less well. Without any, it simply stops.

This is a balanced meal. The fish provides proteins and fats, the potato provides carbohydrates, and the peas and carrots provide vitamins and minerals.

STAY HEALTHY
You should eat three balanced meals every day to keep your body topped up with food and water.

When you are very active, you need to eat plenty of food to keep you going.

People grow quickly in the first twenty years of life. Food provides the body with the nutrients it needs for this.

The food you eat contains different types of **nutrient**. There are foods for energy called **carbohydrates** and **fats**, foods for growth called **proteins**, while **vitamins** and **minerals** keep everything working properly. To make sure that you get all these nutrients, you need to eat many different kinds of food. This creates a balanced diet.

The digestive system

BEFORE FOOD can become useful, you have to break it into tiny pieces that are small enough to enter your body. In other words, your food has to be digested. The parts of the body that do this for you are known as the **digestive system**. This is a series of tubes and bags which mash up the food you have eaten and mix it with chemicals that help to break down the food.

The useful parts of food, called **nutrients**, pass into your blood. Your blood then carries them around your body. Some parts of your food cannot be digested because they are too tough to break down. These leave your body when you go to the toilet.

This apple is about to begin its journey through the body. The digestive system breaks the apple down into nutrients the body can use.

DID YOU KNOW?

Your digestive system turns all the food you eat into a mixture like soup. Whatever you eat — hamburgers, strawberries or chips — looks the same inside your stomach!

Your digestive system is 7-8 metres long, and stretches from your mouth to your rectum. Some sections of it are very long, and are coiled up neatly inside you.

Your **digestive system** starts in your mouth.

Your **oesophagus** is a tube that stretches from your throat to your stomach.

Your **stomach** is a pear-shaped bag that churns up your food.

Your **liver** and **pancreas** are large **organs.** They produce chemicals that help turn your food into mush.

Your **small intestine** is a long wiggly tube which breaks down food and sends nutrients into the blood.

Your **large intestine** is a wider tube at the end of your intestine.

Your **rectum** is the last part of the large intestine. This is where waste materials from the food you have eaten leave your body.

Smelling and tasting

HAVE YOU ever eaten a rotten egg or some mouldy bread? Probably not. That is because your eyes and nose tell you that the food is bad. They do this to protect you from food that can make you ill.

When your stomach is empty, it shrinks and tightens. This creates a feeling we call hunger. It is like an alarm bell telling you to eat.

Your sight and smell also tell you when food is good to eat. Then your mouth starts to make a clear liquid called **saliva** to help make your food moist and easier to eat. But there is one last check your senses make before you swallow any food. **Taste buds** on your tongue check what the food in your mouth tastes like and warn you if it is bad. If you take a mouthful of sour milk, you still have time to spit it out.

DID YOU KNOW?
The senses of smell and taste are very closely linked. When you have a cold, your sense of smell is so poor that you can hardly taste your food.

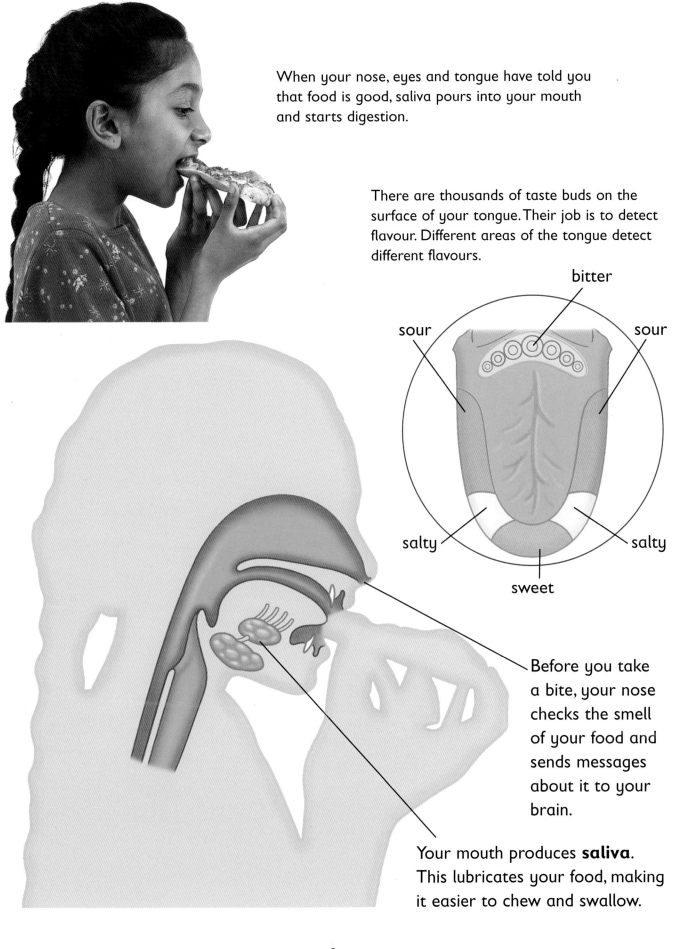

When your nose, eyes and tongue have told you that food is good, saliva pours into your mouth and starts digestion.

There are thousands of taste buds on the surface of your tongue. Their job is to detect flavour. Different areas of the tongue detect different flavours.

bitter

sour

sour

salty

salty

sweet

Before you take a bite, your nose checks the smell of your food and sends messages about it to your brain.

Your mouth produces **saliva**. This lubricates your food, making it easier to chew and swallow.

Chewing your food

W HEN YOU take a bite of food, your mouth breaks it down so you can swallow it. Hard, white teeth along your jaws cut, tear and crush the food, mashing it to a pulp. Your tongue is a powerful muscle that rolls the food around your mouth and mixes it with **saliva**.

Teeth, tongue and saliva work closely together. In less than a minute, they have mashed that mouthful of food into a soft, slippery ball. Your tongue then pushes it towards the back of your mouth. There, the throat muscles squeeze it into the **oesophagus** and the food is swallowed.

STAY HEALTHY
Teeth are damaged by sugar. Protect them by brushing your teeth, visiting the dentist and cutting down on sugary foods.

Sugary foods can damage your teeth and cause the formation of plaque. This is a creamy film where germs can live and spread.

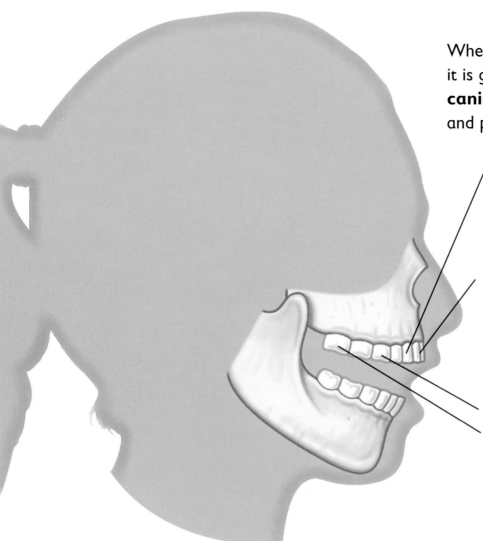

When you bite into a carrot, it is gripped and torn by your **canines** which are sharp and pointed.

Your **incisors** have sharp, straight edges. They are good for slicing and cutting the carrot.

You also have small **premolars** and larger **molars**. These broad, flat teeth are used for chewing and grinding.

You use different types of teeth to help break down food for swallowing. Each type has a different shape and a different use.

DID YOU KNOW?

A circle of muscle inside your lips helps to seal your mouth. This stops you dribbling water and half-chewed bits of food!

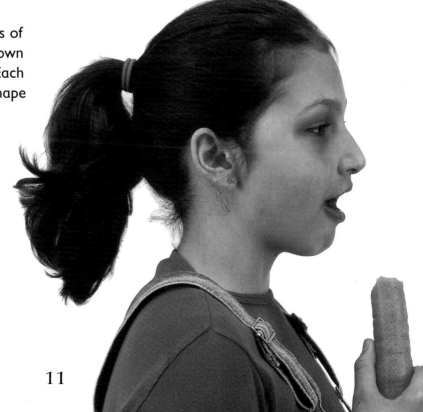

11

Digesting

FOOD THAT has been swallowed soon travels to your **stomach**. This is a large, elastic bag that works rather like a food mixer. It churns up the food with strong digestive juices. These help to break the food down into a thick, sticky soup.

This 'soup' is squirted, little by little, into the **small intestine**. Here, more juices from **organs** called the **liver** and the **pancreas** continue to digest the food. At last, after eight hours or more, the sloppy mix is broken down into tiny parts that your body can absorb.

DID YOU KNOW?
Your intestines squeeze food through the digestive system a bit like toothpaste being squeezed along a tube.

Your stomach needs time to digest a meal before you go for a swim.

STAY HEALTHY
Eating quickly makes your stomach produce a rush of digestive juices. This gives you tummy ache. You can avoid it by eating slowly and chewing each mouthful well.

The first job of your digestive system is to break down food using strong digestive juices from several parts of your body.

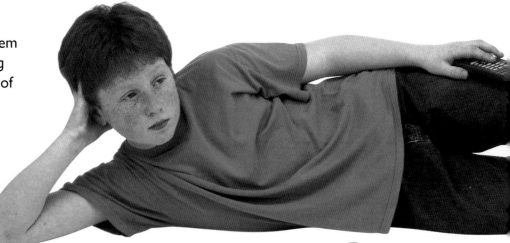

As you swallow, your **oesophagus** squeezes food down to your stomach.

2-3 seconds

Your **stomach** is a bag with thick muscular walls. It mashes up the food and mixes it with digestive juices. The time it takes depends on the type of food.

2-6 hours

Now the food is squirted into your **small intestine**. More digestive juices break down **nutrients** in the food until they are small enough to pass through its walls and into your bloodstream.

1-4 hours

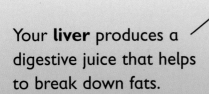

Your **liver** produces a digestive juice that helps to break down fats.

Your **pancreas** produces a powerful digestive juice that flows into the small intestine. It contains chemicals that break down the nutrients in food.

The second job of your digestive system is to soak up water from the food and reject what is left.

The walls of your **large intestine** absorb water from the remains of your food so that what is left becomes more solid.

12–24 hours

DID YOU KNOW?
The large intestine produces a lot of gas – some of it quite smelly. This is made by billions of helpful **bacteria** that live inside you and feed on your leftover food.

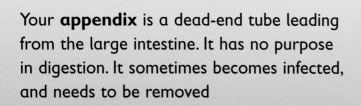

Your **appendix** is a dead-end tube leading from the large intestine. It has no purpose in digestion. It sometimes becomes infected, and needs to be removed

Your **rectum** stores the waste that is left over until you go to the toilet.

2.5 hours

When all the **nutrients** have passed through the walls of your small intestine, a sloppy soup still remains. This is made up of the parts of the food that your body can't use. These now enter your **large intestine**.

The waste moves along very slowly and, as it moves, the walls of the large intestine soak up its water. This leaves the waste drier and more solid. At last, 18 to 36 hours after eating your meal, what's left of the food arrives in your **rectum**. It is stored here until your body gets rid of it by going to the toilet.

STAY HEALTHY
If your large intestine becomes infected you can get diarrhoea. This makes you go to the toilet a lot and makes your body's waste very watery. It is important to drink water to replace the liquid your body has lost.

Your digestive system works more smoothly if your food contains fibre. Fibre is found in fruit, vegetables and wholewheat bread, and cannot be digested. Its job is to add bulk to your food, helping it to move more easily.

A baked potato

POTATOES CONTAIN **carbohydrates**, which help to give you energy. However, carbohydrates need to be digested before they can enter the body. They have to be broken down into a simple form which your body can absorb.

There are two sorts of carbohydrates: sugary ones which you find in cakes and fizzy drinks, and starchy ones. These are in bread, pasta and potatoes.

DID YOU KNOW?
Long-distance runners eat plenty of carbohydrates a few days before a race. The extra fuel keeps their muscles going longer and helps them run faster on the day.

STAY HEALTHY
Try to eat starchy rather than sugary carbohydrates. They give you energy for longer and do less harm to your teeth.

Pasta is a great source of starchy carbohydrates. After eating pasta, you won't feel hungry again for hours.

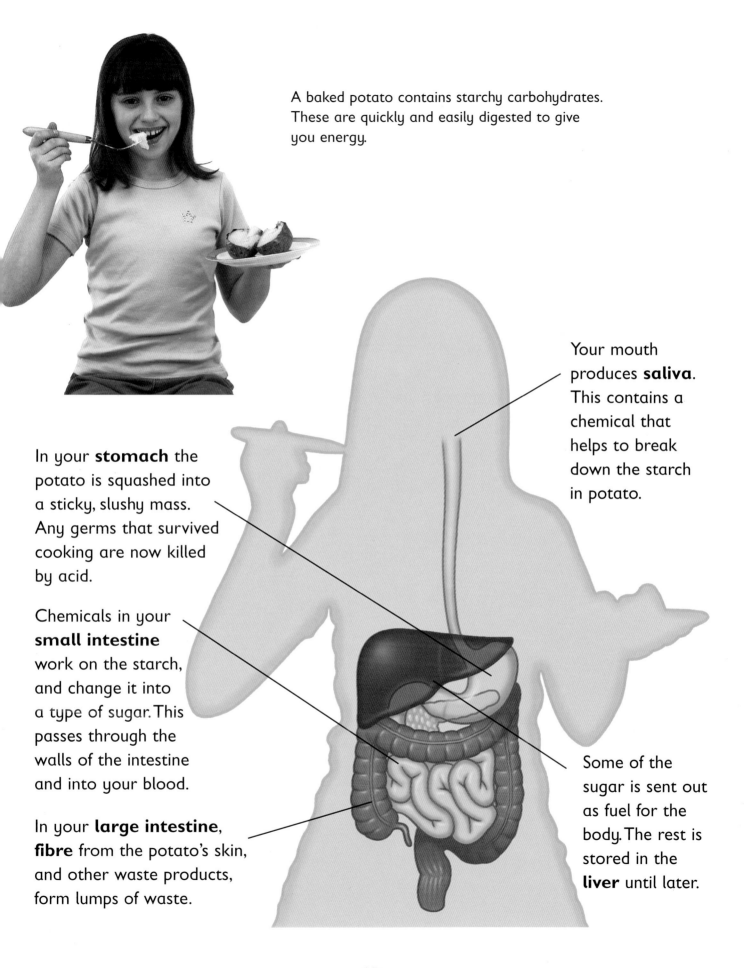

A baked potato contains starchy carbohydrates. These are quickly and easily digested to give you energy.

Your mouth produces **saliva**. This contains a chemical that helps to break down the starch in potato.

In your **stomach** the potato is squashed into a sticky, slushy mass. Any germs that survived cooking are now killed by acid.

Chemicals in your **small intestine** work on the starch, and change it into a type of sugar. This passes through the walls of the intestine and into your blood.

In your **large intestine**, **fibre** from the potato's skin, and other waste products, form lumps of waste.

Some of the sugar is sent out as fuel for the body. The rest is stored in the **liver** until later.

A chicken drumstick

CHICKEN CONTAINS **proteins** and **fats**. The fats are mainly found in the skin, and the proteins in the meat. Proteins help the body to grow and repair damage. They also help to replace worn-out parts. Fats give you energy and help you to grow.

Proteins and fats are complex **nutrients**, and are tricky to digest. Proteins are made up of smaller substances which need to be broken down before your body can use them. Proteins and fats are important nutrients, but you only need to eat a small amount of them to get the goodness they provide.

STAY HEALTHY
Try to eat two portions of protein-rich food every day. Your body cannot store proteins so you need a regular supply.

Proteins are in both plant and animal products. Plants with a lot of protein include grains, **pulses**, nuts and seeds. Animal foods include meat, fish, eggs, cheese and milk.

DID YOU KNOW?
Fats are found in animal foods such as meat, eggs and milk. They are also in plants, but in plants they are called oils.

A chicken drumstick contains both proteins and fats. These nutrients take a long time to digest.

In your **mouth** the chicken is chewed and mixed with saliva. It becomes soft, moist and easy to swallow.

Your **stomach** pounds the chicken to a mush. Chemicals break down the fats and proteins into separate, simpler parts.

Inside your **small intestine**, digestive juices change the fats into tiny droplets. The proteins are also broken down into smaller parts. The nutrients can now pass through your small intestine's walls and seep into your blood.

Water is absorbed from the waste that is left in your **large intestine**.

Blood containing the nutrients passes into your **liver.** Here the proteins are changed into new substances to help your body grow and repair itself. The fats are stored, or sent out as fuel for your body.

Fruit and vegetables

FRUIT AND vegetables contain lots of **vitamins** and **minerals**, which are very important for your body. Vitamins are chemicals that prevent disease and help the body to work properly. Some vitamins are made by the body itself, but others come from your food.

Minerals, such as **calcium** and **iron**, are tiny substances taken up from the soil by plants. Whenever you eat plants (or animals that feed on them), you eat the minerals they contain. Like vitamins, minerals help your body to work properly.

Minerals and vitamins are very important, but you only need them in tiny amounts. They do not need digesting and can pass straight into your blood.

STAY HEALTHY
Try to eat five portions of fruit and vegetables every day. They can be fresh, tinned, frozen or turned into juice.

Fresh fruit and vegetables are packed with vitamins and minerals. The sooner you eat them after they have been picked, the better they are for you.

DID YOU KNOW?
You can fit all the vitamins that you need each day on less than one-eighth of a teaspoon.

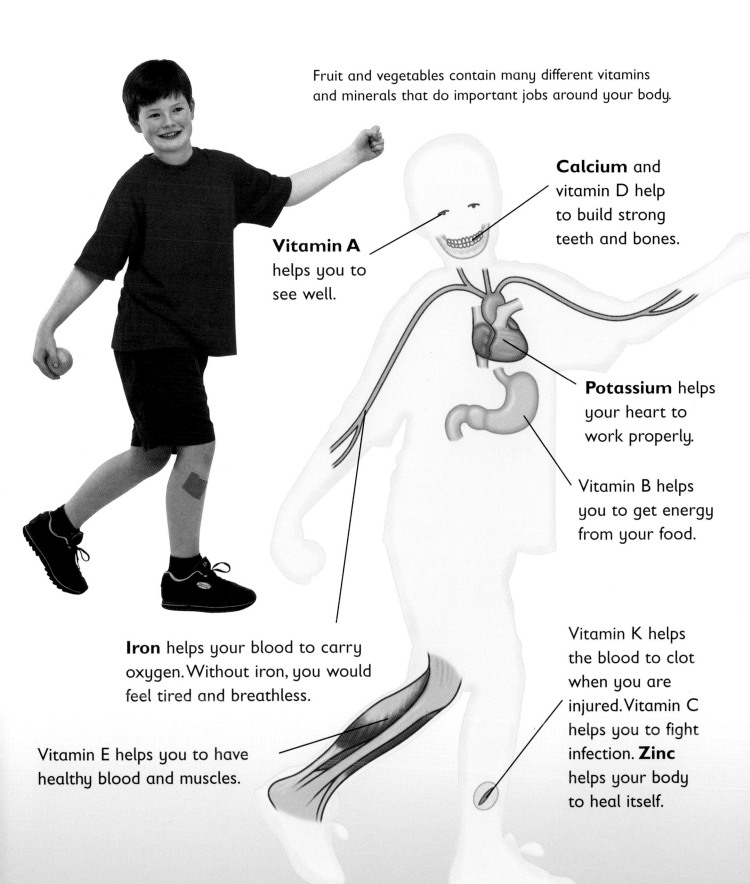

Fruit and vegetables contain many different vitamins and minerals that do important jobs around your body.

Calcium and vitamin D help to build strong teeth and bones.

Vitamin A helps you to see well.

Potassium helps your heart to work properly.

Vitamin B helps you to get energy from your food.

Iron helps your blood to carry oxygen. Without iron, you would feel tired and breathless.

Vitamin K helps the blood to clot when you are injured. Vitamin C helps you to fight infection. **Zinc** helps your body to heal itself.

Vitamin E helps you to have healthy blood and muscles.

A glass of water

WATER IS very important for your body. In fact, you cannot live without it. It makes up over half your body weight and forms the liquids inside you, such as sweat and blood.

Water does not need breaking down inside your body. When you take a gulp of water, it passes straight through your **stomach** and into your **small intestine**. When it reaches your **large intestine**, it passes into your blood.

Blood flows around your body all the time. Every few minutes it arrives at your **kidneys**. The job of your kidneys is to clean your blood by taking out the waste and excess water that your body does not need. This becomes a liquid called **urine**. Urine is stored in your **bladder** until you go to the toilet.

DID YOU KNOW?
Learning to control the muscles in your bladder takes several years. Young children wear nappies until they learn the knack!

People sweat a lot when they exercise. Sweat keeps the body cool and is ninety-nine per cent water.

STAY HEALTHY
You lose water when you breathe, sweat and go to the toilet. You have to replace it by drinking plenty of water – about two litres a day.

Water passes quickly through your digestive system and into your blood.

Water passes straight into your blood from the **large intestine**. This blood flows to your kidneys.

Your **kidneys** filter the blood. They take out waste products and any extra water. The liquid waste, called **urine**, now flows into your bladder.

Blood that has been cleaned of waste products, leaves your kidneys and flows around your body.

Your bladder muscles relax when you go to the toilet.

Your **bladder** gradually fills up with urine. It needs emptying three or four times a day. You do this when you go to the toilet.

Taking care with food

FRESH FOODS, such as meat, fish and cheese, are healthy and delicious. But they are easily spoilt by tiny creatures that live on them. These creatures are too small to see but they are everywhere – on your hands, in the air and on the things you touch. Some are kinds of **fungus** that turn food mouldy. Others are harmful **bacteria** or **germs** and can make you ill.

Germs spread quickly in places that are warm, damp or dirty. They spread more slowly in the cold. That's why fresh foods should be kept in the fridge. Washing your hands and keeping the kitchen clean are other ways to stop germs spreading.

DID YOU KNOW?
Bacteria are not always harmful. Certain good bacteria are added to milk to turn it into yoghurt. These bacteria help us to digest our food better and stop wind.

Fungus on this fruit is turning it mouldy. Food like this is bad to eat and should be thrown away.

Dirty chopping boards, work surfaces and kitchen utensils can spread **germs** to food. Make sure they are clean before you use them.

Germs spread quickly on damp, dirty tea towels. Only use a tea towel if it is clean and dry.

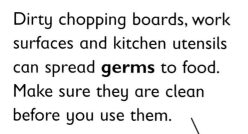

Mould is a **fungus** that spreads through the air and feeds on your food. Eating it can make you ill, so throw mouldy food away.

Washing your hands is important. It stops germs spreading and prevents the illnesses they cause.

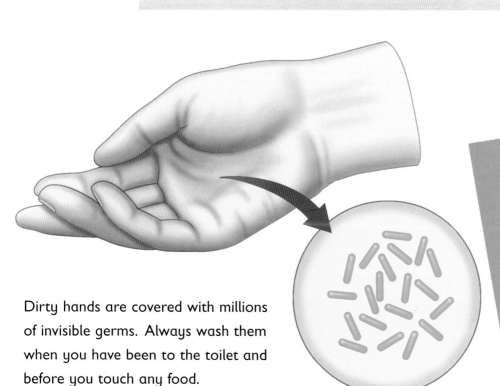

Dirty hands are covered with millions of invisible germs. Always wash them when you have been to the toilet and before you touch any food.

STAY HEALTHY
Always keep food covered. This stops flies from landing on it. Flies feed on things like dogs' muck and dead animals and carry lots of germs.

Food allergies

SOMETIMES YOUR body reacts badly to certain foods. This is called a food **allergy**. The body mistakes the food for a harmful substance, and reacts to fight it. This can cause skin rashes, sickness or **diarrhoea**. At its worst the reaction can be life-threatening.

People do not always know which food is causing the reaction. Doctors discover it by doing skin tests. They make a row of tiny pinpricks on your body and inject small amounts of suspect foods. If you are allergic to one of the foods, the pinprick will swell and turn red. This means you must not eat that food again. It can be hard in the case of milk, eggs, wheat or nuts, because they are used in many foods. Children may not be able to eat food at parties in case it makes them ill.

STAY HEALTHY
If you have a bad allergic reaction to a food you may need medicine or an injection from a doctor. Some people carry their own injection kits to use in an emergency. If anyone you know has a bad reaction to food, always dial 999 and call an ambulance.

Wheat, nuts, milk, eggs and shellfish are some of the foods that can cause an allergic reaction.

DID YOU KNOW?
Nuts can cause powerful allergic reactions. That is why packets carry a warning label to tell you if the food inside may contain traces of nuts.

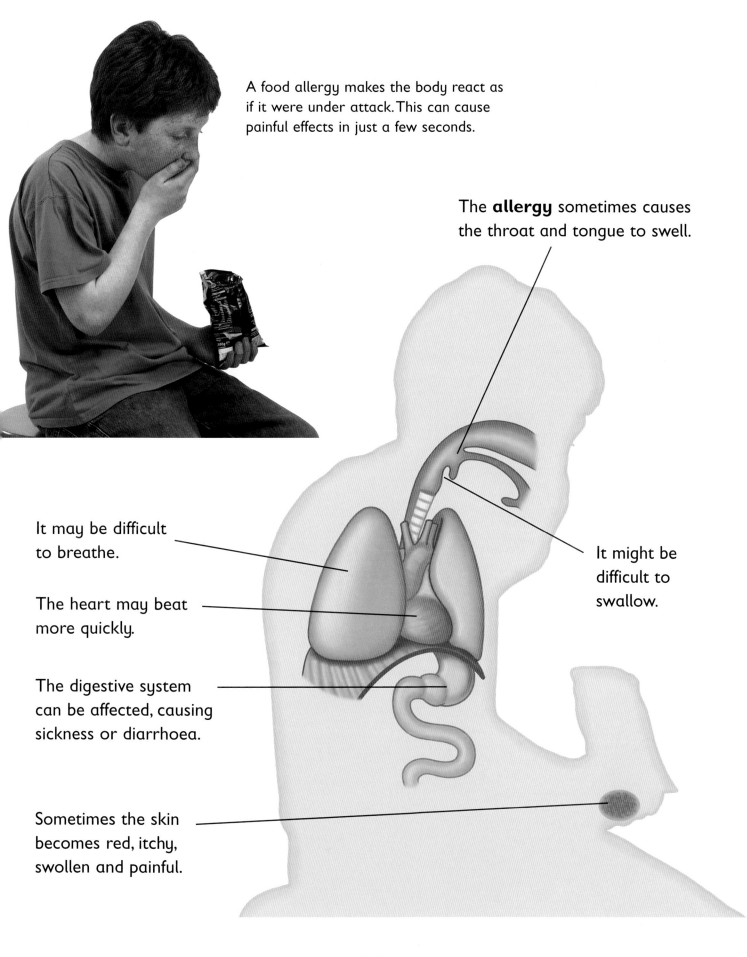

A food allergy makes the body react as if it were under attack. This can cause painful effects in just a few seconds.

The **allergy** sometimes causes the throat and tongue to swell.

It might be difficult to swallow.

It may be difficult to breathe.

The heart may beat more quickly.

The digestive system can be affected, causing sickness or diarrhoea.

Sometimes the skin becomes red, itchy, swollen and painful.

Healthy eating

YOUR BODY needs many different **nutrients**. You can only get them all by eating a variety of foods. This is called a balanced diet. It is best to avoid too many sugary foods, such as biscuits and sweets, because they can rot your teeth. You should also avoid too many fatty foods, such as pizzas and chips. It won't harm you to eat them now and then, but too many can make you fat.

Everyone needs to eat the right amount of food for their own body. Children need to eat more than older people. Somebody big usually needs to eat more than somebody small. Eating too much can make you overweight. Eating too little will starve your body of the nutrients it needs.

It is easy to eat plenty of different foods on a picnic. Choose juicy strawberries and grapes as well as sandwiches and crisps.

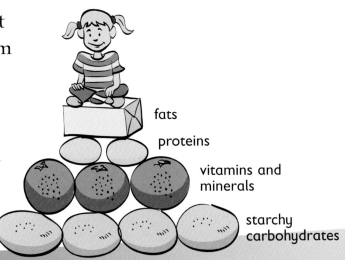

fats

proteins

vitamins and minerals

starchy carbohydrates

STAY HEALTHY
This food pyramid shows all the foods and nutrients your body needs. You should eat plenty of the foods at the base of the pyramid but only a little of the ones at the top.

Fruit and vegetables provide you with **vitamins**, **minerals** and **fibre**.

Milk supplies your bones and teeth with **calcium**.

Try to eat many different kinds of food. They are good for you in different ways.

Meat, fish, eggs and nuts contain **proteins**.

Bread, cereals, pasta and rice contain **carbohydrates**.

DID YOU KNOW?

You don't have to eat meat to get all the protein and iron you need. You can get protein from beans, chickpeas, lentils, milk, cheese and eggs. Iron can be provided by spinach, watercress and other leafy greens, and by dried fruits.

A gooey cream cake makes a fabulous treat. We all love foods like this now and then!

Glossary

allergy A reaction by your body to a particular food. It may cause sickness.

appendix A short dead-end tube off your large intestine. It has no purpose in digestion.

bacteria Tiny living things that are too small to see. Some have useful roles in the body but others can make you ill.

bladder A bag-like organ where urine is stored.

calcium A mineral in foods such as milk and cheese. It helps to build strong bones and teeth.

canine Any of the four sharp, pointed teeth near the front of your mouth.

carbohydrate A nutrient that gives your body energy. It is found in starchy or sugary foods such as bread, pasta, rice and biscuits.

digestive system A series of tubes and bags which break down the food you eat so that it can be used by the body

fats Nutrients that give your body energy. They are found in foods that contain oil, butter and margarine.

fibre The coarse, thread-like bits found in potato skins, carrots and other foods.

fungus Tiny living things that turn your food mouldy.

germs Harmful bacteria that can cause disease.

incisor Any of the four front teeth which have a straight cutting edge.

iron A mineral found in foods such as spinach and liver. Iron helps your blood to carry oxygen.

kidneys Two organs that turn waste products from your blood into urine.

large intestine The final part of your digestive system where waste products become more solid.

liver An organ which produces a digestive juice to help digestion, but also takes in nutrients from foods and releases them to your body.

mineral A substance such as calcium and iron that is found in the soil and the foods we eat.

molar The broad, flat teeth at the back of your mouth that crush and grind food.

nutrient Any part of a food that gives your body the energy or goodness it needs to grow.

oesophagus The tube that joins your throat to your stomach.

organ Any part of your body that has a special job to do, such as your liver.

pancreas An organ near your stomach that produces juices that help to digest your food.

potassium A mineral found in foods such as broccoli and spinach. It helps to keep your heart and brain healthy.

premolar The small, flat teeth behind your canines that help to crush and grind your food.

protein A nutrient that helps your body to grow and repair itself.

pulses The seeds of plants such as beans, peas and lentils that can be dried and used as food.

rectum The part of your body where solid waste is stored before it leaves the body.

saliva The watery juice made in your mouth that helps you chew and break down food.

small intestine The longest part of your digestive system where food is broken down into useful nutrients, which are then absorbed by your body.

stomach The bag where the food you swallow is mashed up and mixed with digestive juices.

taste buds The parts of your tongue that detect flavour in food.

urine The yellow liquid waste that is produced by your body.

vitamin A special substance found in food, which your body needs in tiny amounts to stay healthy. There are lots of different vitamins such as vitamin A and vitamin C. Each has a special job to do.

zinc A mineral that helps your body to heal.

Useful information

Books

Eating by Anna Sandeman, from the "Your Body" series (Franklin Watts, 2000)

Look at Your Digestion by Steve Parker, from the "Look at Your Body" series (Franklin Watts, 1996)

Disgusting Digestion by Nick Arnold in the "Horrible Science" series (Hippo, 1998)

Why Do I Vomit And Other Questions About Digestion by Angela Royston, from the "Body Matters" series (Heinemann, 2002)

Websites

www.brainpop.com/health/digestive/digestion
Contains a short film about the digestive system

www.bbc.co.uk/health/nutrition/basics_digestive
.shtml
Good visuals and lots of basic information

www.sciencenet.org.uk/
Read the answers to questions sent in by other website users. Food and Digestion questions appear under Biology and Medical Science. Answers are presented in three levels, ranging from the very simple to the more complicated.

www.schoolmenu.com
A fun and informative website, with games, puzzles and facts.

www.educationworld.com/a_sites/sites010.shtml
Contains links to other useful websites.

Organisations

British Nutrition Foundation
High Holborn House
52-54 High Holborn
London WC1V 6RQ
www.nutrition.org.uk
Provides information and advice about healthy eating.

British Allergy Foundation
Deepdene House
30 Bellegrove Road
Welling
Kent
DA16 3PY
www.allergyfoundation.com
Provides information and support for people with allergies.

Eating Disorders Association (EDA)
Wensum House
103 Prince of Wales Road
Norwich
Norfolk
NR1 1DW
www.edauk.com
Provides information and support for people with eating disorders.

Index